spring

ample feast

Barbara,
We've heard such
good things about you
from Donna.
I hope some of these
poems strike a chord.

Warm regards,

Bill

william danis

for teresa, with love

"He does a good work, who pausing in the way,
calls to the feverish crowd that in [the] life
we live upon this beautiful earth,
there may, after all, be something vaster and better
than dress and table, and business, and politics."

Walt Whitman, 1851

the eve of the first day of spring:
the tree outside my window waits for leaves
around its base tender crocus spikes
struggle through the last of the winter snow
on the sidewalk, a woman pauses to
unbutton her heavy winter coat and then is gone
the line between the darkened roofs
and the darkening sky grows less distinct
a dog, far off, begins to howl
across the street, a man pulls down a shade
and with it goes the final light
alone, caught between the ending day
and the descending night,
I sit and wait and howl without a sound
something's being born; something has to die.

I am that which I seek:
a name, a word, a sound
a breathing held within
released with ease profound
a wind to match the raging fire
burning brighter, burning higher

I take communion with the trees
of pine and oak and bending birch
this mountain is my daily bread
this forest is my food and church

I need no altar, statue, steeple
my salvation's not in other people
but in overwhelming ocean's might
the sight of endless stars at night

I am who am abides in me
abides in flower, insect, tree
asks not that I kneel to pray
insists not that there's just one way

I need no rabbi, priest or preacher
this sunlight is my sage and teacher
guiding me till day has passed
and I am safely home at last

I take communion with the trees
of pine and oak and bending birch
this mountain is my daily bread
this forest is my food and church

poet:

prism of mouth music
humming verb refractor
filter of spoken rainbow
silent song extractor

mirror of eye music
rhyming view reflector
deflector of sight song
singing scene projector

light conductor, ever bending
sound director, never ending

barking dog and straying cow
seldom laying hen
clouded sky and drying rain
mown grass grown again
broken horse and fallen bird
darkly fading light
hissing cat and brazen sheep
assure what's left is right

bread baking:
when the kitchen work's complete
and the kneaded dough's at rest
comes a thought I would repeat
that the rising shows it best:
though we serve a different dish
still we are indeed divine
apostles of a flawless fish
disciples of a perfect wine

sunlight-shading olive tree
chanting softly calls to me
entrancing me with green
sunlight shining child, ayard
laughter amplified by wind
encircles now to out the glow
and hold the stranger in
cloud banks that float gently by
whistle to the humming sky
tunes to trap the passer-by
as soaring bird with sun afire
sings the vision brighter, higher

stones that block the river's run
clouds that trap the racing sun
earth that stays the push of seed
fence that slows the rabbit's speed
obstacles that slow the race
channels that increase the pace

some say time's an empty plate
missing cup, forgotten date
some say time's a broken bowl
misplaced spoon, abandoned goal
I say time's a thing that bakers bake
a piece of thickly frosted layer cake
life's dessert, abundant in the breeze
another slice of sky-cloud-tree-grass-water, please.

I was talking to a bird one day
asking if he knew the way
when I thought I heard my neighbor say of me
"the man's talking to a tree!"

while apologizing to my lawn
whose tiny limbs I'd trampled on
I heard my neighbor whisper 'round
"he's talking to the ground!"

I was warmly thanking blazing sun
for doing the fine job he'd done
when I thought I heard my neighbor sigh
"now he's talking to the sky!"

who know the game? who makes the rules?
all things the same, we're equal fools

summer

rolling sand dunes catching morning light
steaming sea waves cooling ocean's might
dancing sea stones resting still on beach
waving sea grass staying sandy reach
fleeing seagulls framing steady sun
constant tide, ephemeral day begun

my muse is back in rehab
what's she thinking?
that booze and pills
can douse the fiery pain,
end the endless ennui
the mire in melancholy
the explosion of emotions?

truth be told, she's not thinking
as usual, she's feeling
that's her problem
can she be saved from herself?
can she ever learn to control
the outbursts, to equalize
the highs and lows?

good luck to her
I am doing all I can to
undermine her recovery,
to bait and irritate, infuriate,
agitate, exacerbate I must
God knows her redemption
would be the death of me

I long to climb the cliffs
of Singing Beach and
feel the summer sun
within my reach
the ocean's magic mirror
crystal blue
reflecting all the love
I feel for you

I long to lie upon
the highest stone
the two of us as one
we two alone
your shining love reflecting
love from me
above the flow of
roaring, shining sea

I long to climb the cliffs
of Singing Beach
and feel your glowing sun
within my reach
beneath the endless dome
of cloudless blue
as endless as the love
I feel for you

lighthouse:
faithful night disciple
spinning light
permanent apostle
whirling, bright
dancing deacon
constant, strong
steady beacon,
moving song

there's a joy in running
parting water, easing out
there's a calm in smoothly moving
one in rhythm with the waves
there's a peace in silent
sailing on a never-ending sea
that's shining mirror bright
flying, floating, falling
outward, inward into light

poetry makes demands
now don't get me wrong
it's not mountains
it's more lakes
or, better yet, ocean
you cannot help but want
to wander in
wetness binds
in a weird way:
the silent seascape
entices you to wade in
lured by the siren's unheard song
to float in your own fashion
in a quiet little pool

sunrise:
the huge orange wafer rises slowly
from an horizon steeped in steel-gray morning mist
to rend the nighttime's shroud of black
and spark a host of fleeting crimson fires
whose brilliant embers dance and die
on clouds and trees and blazing sky
while shining sea birds whisper to the breeze
a new rebirth of earth's viaticum

words are hollow things
jetsam that some wave may bring
tumbled shells washed up on beach
left to struggle now to reach
some safer, higher ground to hide
beyond the grasp of drowning tide

words are empty things
flotsam that some sea may bring
shells to scratch a message in the sand
hieroglyphics to help us understand
that the tide that batters you and me
is the self same tide that sets us free

bar fish
sinking far fish
brined in booze fish
ready for the cruise fish
never wander very far fish
deeper water much too far fish
drowning in the blues fish
tails, you lose fish
fallen star fish
bar fish

flapping flight of shrieking gulls
crash and crunch of scattered shells
howl of wind through shifting dune
nature's sweet, discordant tune
roar outside the din of human reach
silent summer sunset on the beach

autumn

her garlands twined in rue and columbine
mad autumn twists and tears the tender vine
delights in dappling whiskered peaches
blighting all within her reaches
then to satisfy some inner need
explodes the perfect rose to seed
still longing for her melancholy Dane
content she's manifest her pain
she sails from bending bough to water's deep
to drift away in dark and dreamless sleep

decaying cabin in the woods
empty now but full for good
broken windows streaming light
missing doors that still invite
smokeless chimney warming nests
hollow floor where rodents rest
discarded homestead, wooden rind
something's fruit, something's find

a woman with a bunch of flowers
sat beside me on the train
and stared outside to where
the clouded sky was shedding rain
and a weaker of the roses
shed a petal on the seat
to lie between us in the space
where strangers seldom meet
and like that petal I was lost
like that sky was overcast
saddened by the revelation
that neither rain nor roses last

the light poured in
through the green glass
and swam in her hair
alone, asleep on the crowded bus
she did not know
that I swam in her shadow
there beside her
and knew her well
before she awoke
and spilled into the light

abandoned farm
deserted pines
clouded skies
fallen lines
leveled fence
rusted well
opened gate
silent bell
tossed wagon
tumbled load
beaten path
traveled road

my light bulb burns at both ends
the filament is firing itself cold
the incandescent heating
exploding sparks receding
implodes the fragile light
scatters dying embers
to light the cold dark night

rain wet streets
where strangers meet
but seldom intersect

inviting doors closed and locked
to ward off lonely stranger's knock
and send him on his way

windowpanes reflecting light
on strangers held at bay at night
by sashes closed and locked

merging paths, diverging ways
warming hearths, chilling days

we are the shopping mall people
you can see it in our faces
you can see it in our eyes
barely looking, staring blankly
waiting weakly for an opening
waiting meekly on the clock

we are the shopping mall people
you can see it in our faces
you can see it in our smiles
feigned and frozen, spent on
objects concealing hidden prices
paid with minutes of our lives

we are the shopping mall people
you can see it in our faces
how the whole reveals the cost:
while we trade our souls for solace
for the things that seem to matter
time is wasted, we are lost

failing rose that holds fast to the bush
aging bird that makes the southern rush
autumn leaf that will not float the breeze
dying man whose fighting will not cease
lament for creatures leveled after all
praise for creatures rising with the fall

spotted apples spilled around
broken branches on the ground
dying, gourd-entwining vines
caught in crossed and crooked lines
nuts from leafless limbs of trees
shaken by November breeze
berries left on broken bush
abandoned in the autumn rush
meal for squirrel, rabbit, bird
less seldom seen, less seldom heard
for those discerning most from least
sufficient banquet, ample feast

winter

blazing sunlight explosions
crackling crystal implosions
thermal dance of frozen dew
bursting through:
snowflakes melted dry
wet vapor beads for icy winter sky

red bird rests
on leafless limb of ash
framed by sloping roof
of blue-black slate
above the running lines
of dark electric wires
whose dancing shadows fall
on fields of winter white
blazing bird:
bright-shining stroke to stretch
the canvas paper thin
tiny sun
to draw the world within

the soft-spoken woman in the antique shop
entraps me in her endless monologue
in her sad tales of death and dying
her friend in the recent car accident
her brother last year of throat cancer
her father of old age and dementia
"his bones was so brittle near the end
he broke his hip with one slip on the floor"

I shift and look away as if to leave
but still she drones on and on
nervously buttoning her heavy
coat in the too warm store
perhaps to mask the acrid smell
of monthly blood she seeks to hide

in spite of my want to leave
I begin to drift, entangled in her sanguine spell
mesmerized, entranced, entrapped
I see in her grey eyes the glassy
eye of the dead fish I've come upon
unexpectedly on the quiet beach
the shriveled, unpicked zinnias
standing far off, stiff and broken
in the drifted snow in my backyard
the utter stillness of the small field mouse
the neighbor's cat has left on my back steps
the rotted apples, puckered, frozen
out of reach on the upper branches
of the leafless tree near the barn

I drift deeper and deeper into her
until suddenly alarmed, aware
of my own drowning I struggle to resist
force myself to consciousness
reject the silent soothing sleep
her vampire spell invites

I mumble some cliché about the time
stumble blindly out the door
rush down the steps
and toward the safety of my truck
gulping in the bitter winter air
grateful that I've managed to escape
knowing that there's no escape
as the sinking afternoon sun
turns the distant gray horizon
the lifeless color of dried blood

songscape of a mid-December day:
hum of dawn on fields of snowy white
chirp of bird alight in leafless tree
howl of solo hound in far off field
wheeze and whistle of the rushing wind
scrape and tap of shovel's steady beat
whine of engine idles keeping time
discordant morning voices, soothing winter rhyme

jagged rocks smoothly strewn afield
akimbo limbs of geometric trees
wise rabbit tracks crazy in the snow
streaming water stilled by winter's freeze
resting bird arched for ready flight
sunlight blazing on a chilly day
all things contradictory, bent
make straight the crooked way

the news of your impending death
meant nothing to me
another phone call on a busy day

I had no intention of seeing you
or taking any note of your passing
all these years after my escape
from your tightly clamped vise

but when I learned that you
were in the final coma
I felt the need to see
the monster one last time
road kill come to see its maker

so here you are, old man
terror of my youth
reduced to this
shrunk to half your size
and turned to paste

the flesh hangs off
your once muscled arm
(all the better to beat me with)
in rubbery folds

bony, hairless white legs
stick out from your
wrinkled hospital johnny
toenails thick and crusty

I've traveled here to say
I hate you, old man
not with the seething rage
and want to kill that
owned me for so long

but with a numb
and distant hate that is
the final fading residue of
my forgetting you

here is my final prayer for you,
old man
may your spirit's passing
be lonely and painful and slow
and may it wander
troubled and tormented
until the last bitter light of you is out

there is no excuse for you
for the meanness and the destruction
and damage that you wrought

once when I was eight or nine
and you were beating me
I cried out that you weren't my father
and you beat me all the harder

beat me in an explosion of rage
to prove that you owned me
and I had no right to recoil
you nearly killed me
but saved me for another day

so I have come to tell you this, old man
now that you can no longer hurt me:
you are not my father
and have never been
and I will somehow learn to forgive you
with this battered heart that is
as cold and indifferent to you
as you are now to me

a spirit seeks its secret path
in multitudes of ways
from calm and reasoned disbelief
to wild, ecstatic praise
a spirit seeks its unity
it will not do without
if all indeed are born in sin
in death all are born out

I helped a holy woman
breathe her last breath,
die in peace
it was thunder
it was lightning
it was roaring rain
that even as it fell
was changed to sunlight
radiant, streaming, rousing
wild and reckless ocean
an explosion blinding, brilliant
in the darkness of the mourning
a joining and a breaking
a sleeping and a waking

I ask the master of the world
what it is I am to do
to join the voices, soothing, strong
harmonize my single song

and the answer that comes humming
through a sea of light it seems
sings the foolishness of asking
and the emptiness of dreams

the master of the spirit world
tells me how to spend my days:
singing songs of mute thanksgiving
singing songs of silent praise

I smiled twice before I died
once for peace, once for pride
I sighed, then sighed again
first for me, then for man
but those sighs released a laugh
echoed both ways on the path
I smiled twice before I died
once for peace, once for pride